A Child's Story of
Easter

By Etta Wilson
Illustrated by Mary Ann Utt

ISBN 0-8249-5365-7

Published by Ideals Children's Books, An imprint of Ideals Publications, A division of Guideposts
535 Metroplex Drive, Suite 250, Nashville, Tennessee 37211
www.idealspublications.com

Printed and bound in Mexico by RR Donnelley & Sons.

Library of Congress CIP data on file

1 0 8 6 4 2   3 5 7 9

ideals children's books™
Nashville, Tennessee

Lilies are the flowers of spring and of Easter. Their white blossoms with bright yellow throats seem to sing a song of welcome to the new season and especially to the Easter holiday.

Easter is the day that we celebrate God's greatest gift to the world: His Son, Jesus Christ.

Jesus liked to see the lilies blooming in the springtime. He once said to His followers, "Look at the lilies. See how beautiful they are. If God dresses the flowers of the field so beautifully, then you do not have to worry about what to wear.

"God knows you need clothes to wear and food to eat. If you will just set your mind on doing what God wants, He will always take care of you."

Jesus taught people about God, and He performed many miracles. He healed the sick. He brought those who had died back to life.

Wherever He went, Jesus told people about God's love.

But some men were very powerful, and they were afraid they would lose their power if the people followed Jesus. So, they began watching Jesus very closely.

Jesus had a special group of followers called disciples. They traveled with Jesus as He went back and forth across the land. More and more people began to listen to Jesus' teachings, to believe Him, and to follow Him.

One day, in early spring, Jesus came into the city of Jerusalem, riding on a small donkey. Great crowds gathered to greet Him, cheering as He passed. Some spread leafy palm branches across the road, making a carpet for Him to ride upon. They waved their arms and shouted, "Hosanna! Hosanna! Blessed is He who comes in the name of the Lord!"

All the while, the chief priests and the elders watched and listened. They wondered how they could get rid of Jesus.

Jesus rode through the streets of Jerusalem and went straight to the temple. Many people had gathered there to worship. But when Jesus saw that the moneychangers were buying and selling in the temple and not using it as a place of worship, He became very angry.

"You thieves!" Jesus shouted. "You are making God's house into a robber's cave!"

Then He took a whip and drove the moneychangers out of the temple.

The chief priests and the elders were furious when they heard about this. They were so angry with Jesus that they began plotting to kill Him.

For several days, Jesus and His disciples came and went from Jerusalem. Every day, Jesus taught in the temple. He spoke more and more boldly each time. The chief priests and the elders asked Him many questions. They tried to trick Him into saying something that was against the Jewish laws. But Jesus knew they were trying to trap Him.

One of Jesus' disciples was named Judas. He was in charge of the group's money. Judas wanted Jesus to be rich and powerful, like a king, but Jesus kept giving everything away. Judas became so angry with Jesus that he decided to help the chief priests trap Him.

On the Thursday before Passover, which is an important holiday for the Jewish people, Jesus took His disciples to a room that He had borrowed for the special feast.

While the food was being served, Jesus got up. He wrapped a towel around His waist and poured water in a bowl. Then He began to wash the disciples' feet. When He finished, He said, "Let this be an example to you. Just as I have washed your feet, so you should wash each other's feet."

Later, as they ate, Jesus looked around at the disciples and said, "One of you here is going to betray me." They all stared at one another and wondered who it could be—all except Judas, who quickly got up and left.

After they had finished eating, Jesus led the disciples out to a garden, which was called the Garden of Gethsemane. "Wait here while I go to pray to my Father," Jesus told them.

Jesus had just returned to the disciples when Judas came into the garden. He was leading a group of soldiers who carried swords and clubs. They seized Jesus, and the disciples ran away in fear.

The soldiers took Jesus to the house of the Jewish high priest, where false charges were made against Him. They then took Him to Pilate, the Roman governor, and claimed that Jesus was trying to be a king. Pilate agreed to sentence Jesus to death on a cross. It was a terrible way to die.

The next day, Jesus carried the heavy cross to the place where He was to die. The soldiers wove a crown of thorns and laughed as they put it on His head. Jesus' hands and feet were nailed to the cross, and He was left to die.

Even though it was the middle of the day, the sun stopped shining. In the darkness, the earth rumbled, the ground shook, and the rocks burst open. Then, Jesus died.

One of Jesus' followers, Joseph of Arimathea, got permission to take Jesus' body and bury Him. Joseph placed the body in a new tomb that had been cut out of the rock. He then rolled a large stone in front of the opening to the tomb while some of the women watched.

Early on Sunday morning, just after sunrise, some women went down to the tomb. One of them was named Mary Magdalene. She was surprised to see that the stone had been rolled away and the tomb was open! Mary thought someone had stolen Jesus' body, so she ran back to tell the disciples.

Mary found John and Peter, and the three of them raced back to the tomb. The disciples saw that it was empty and went back to their homes. Mary stayed near the tomb, crying. Two angels appeared and said, "Why are you crying?"

"They have taken my Lord away," she said. But as she turned around, she saw Jesus standing right before her!

"Mary," He said, "go and tell my brothers that I am alive."

Mary ran back to the disciples as fast as she could. But when she told them the wonderful news, they didn't believe her!

Later that same night, the disciples were gathered in the home of one of Jesus' followers. They had locked all the doors because they were still afraid of the chief priests who had killed Jesus.

Suddenly Jesus appeared among them and said, "Peace be with you." The disciples saw Him with their own eyes, and they were filled with joy. Jesus was alive! He had risen from the grave!

Jesus said to them, "Go and spread the Gospel to the world. Tell everyone that those who believe in me and are baptized will be saved."

Ever since that time, every spring at Easter, people all over the world celebrate the wonderful news that Jesus is alive. They go to worship at sunrise, church bells ring, and the Easter lilies bloom. It is a time to laugh and sing. New life has come to the world.